Regards of the
Author.

Back Talk

Back Talk

Poems by
Reese Alsop

1980

William L. Bauhan, Publisher
DUBLIN, NEW HAMPSHIRE

Library of Congress Cataloguing in Publication data:
Alsop, Reese Fell.
  Back talk.
  I. Title.
PS3551.L73B3   811'.54   80-10084
ISBN 0-87233-053-2

PRINTED IN THE UNITED STATES OF AMERICA

FOR

Lee, Brooke, Elise, Jane, Anne and Penn

Contents

8

Introduction

WHEN I was a boy we had a hired man who used to say, "Don give me any of your back talk."

Poetry is back talk against the universe. It demands quiet, stillness, cessation of the geometric progression of stimuli. It insists upon time to really work, to carve out a rock, a monument which states unequivocally "behold and wonder." Here is something beautiful, momentous and unchanging.

What is to follow is a mixed bag which arrived over a thirty year stretch like small explosions, demanding attention. Most of them fulfill Robert Frost's postulates that "A poem should run a course from delight to wisdom, like a piece of ice on a hot stove ride on its own melting." A few don't.

Anyway, here they are. I hope you like them.

Back Talk

In March

It's different in March.
The face lashing and wind that turn your back
   to the storm,
Are gone. The unhurried snowflakes are large now,
   and falling straight,
Making fragile ladyfingers out of twigs and vines.
The hemlocks mope under their load,
And the western sun is really trying. You can see
   light behind a cloud.
And visibility survives, across a field to where
   an apple orchard secretly plans
Another kind of white to haunt, another twilight
   later on.

Two A. M. Housecall

There ran in front of my car one night
A cat that was black with a dash of white,
Lean, and long and debonair
Intent upon something that wasn't there,
Like a man obsessed with a single goal,
Such as winning a race, or saving a soul.
Though he changed my course and checked my speed,
While paying me never the slightest heed,
And the impact of his peregrinations
Altered arrival of medications,
Our paths had crossed and who's to say
Which one of us had the right of way?

A Defector's Manifesto

I'm a filthy American Imperialist Capitalist.
My methods for making dough are the rapidist.
I'm so stupid, conniving, defective and vain
I've been known to get up from my seat in a train,
To give to a lady who'd not even asked.
I even believe in a thing called the past.
My hair is cut short, and I'm properly dressed.
My diction and speech can compare with the best.
My shoes are both shined, and I walk with a gait
Fantastically snappy, outrageously straight.
I'm likely to take off my hat when I meet
A lady who's passing me by in the street.
In fact, I'm depraved, with a hideous quirk,
I'm happy and healthy and keen on my work.

Still Life

If you pick forsythia in March,
And put them in water, and place them in a window in the sun,
They bloom before their time,
Like a girl who stepped outside the normal run of things to
    find her love.
They both discover grief.
In one the tears are pearls, the other yellow shavings on the rug.
And both are strangers to a storm.
They stand together, looking out the window at the snow.

Socrates

You have to be willing to walk on ahead a little way
  into the dark,
Remembering beauty seen, glory known, and the
  spark.
You have to be willing to give up the policy, the
  insurance, the compensation due,
Sustained by love, and holding to what is true.

They Know

I

The daffodils arriving first,
Survey the scene before the burst
Of bud or leaf or red or gold.
For them the earth is bleak and old
The wind is rough. The air is cold.

II

They turn their faces to the sun
To trace the arc each day must run,
Innocent, fresh beside the pond,
Like girls with yellow bonnets on.
Is their beauty sure and safe
Because they take the spring on faith?

Punctuation

The morning storm produces the thunder and the rain.
A gust of wind blows through the house and disappears again,
Leaving behind a statement that it has gone before,
The faraway, emphatic, sudden slamming of a door.

Pyramus and Thisbe

I

The space between our rooms was small
No thicker than two hands,
And yet the veto was enough
To counter love's demands

II

Her head at night lay very near
To where my own reclined,
But still the wall could interdict
Whatever the heart inclined.

III

The architect had laid his plans
Three hundred years before,
To build a solid edifice,
And make a squeaky floor.

IV

He had not understood my need
To move as on thin ice,
Along the boards where nothing less
Than silence would suffice.

V

If genius is the capacity,
For taking infinite pains,
My rate of progress through the night
Entitles me to same.

VI

In fact my expertise was such,
I'd bumped a rocking chair,
Before she heard, turned the light,
And found me standing there.

VII

I think she'd been expecting me.
I think she had surmised.
Her smile was apprehensive but,
She did not look surprised.

Goodbye

What it means to them and means to me
To see twin girls run under a tree,
Over the dew and across the lawn
To wave goodbye in the early morn,
Is different because their age is three,
And mine's sufficient for reverie.

Twenty-Fifth Reunion

What will you settle for after the first quarter?
Is it the colonnaded white elephant
With the kind of security in the bank
That rises and falls with the tide?
Or is it the little-boy dream of the boat and the
Bottle of Whiskey,
Drifting endlessly and lazily with the trades?
Or does the exclusiveness of clubs and coteries
Shield you from the storm?
No. To be weary, with sweat in my eyes,
And love in my heart, to be laughing,
I will settle only for these.

"Oh Mistress Mine"
Fiftieth Reunion: "Medicine is a Jealous Mistress"—Osler

Glancing across her shoulder once again,
Your jealous mistress, fifty years in flight,
Pursued beyond long avenues of pain,
Demanding, harsh, insistent in the night,
Bestows her bounty with a generous hand,
Only to steadfast labor, and intent,
Her gifts the polished discipline of mind,
The dignity of skill, the heart content.
Aristocratic company she keeps,
Yielding herself to that peculiar breed,
That promises no matter what it reaps
To render service in accord with need,
Until at last she guides the ship aright
Across the bar, beyond the farthest light.

Reflections through a Rear View Mirror, Darkly.

I

Myself when young did have some fun
And drove without compunction,
One hand on the steering wheel
And one in close conjunction,
Wrapped around the lady's waist,
To flirt with and confound her,
A bit of a cad, a buccaneer, a playboy and a bounder.

II

Young men today mirabilé
Are not like me and you.
With mien serene, they drive their queen
To where she's going to.
Both hands are anchored to the wheel
With firmness and decor,
Quite useless for the purposes as mentioned heretofore.

III

The chick today makes all the play
She's groovy and she's cool,
And what she's doing to that square
She learned in Public School.
Both arms are wrapped around his neck
She's halfway in his lap,
What I can't see is how can he
Not figure what she's at.

25

A Sense of Direction

The thrush who found our lifeline in the dawn,
Put himself down as if the ship were his,
With tail a squared off pointing towards the sky,
And posture set to tell it like it is.

He flew around and sat behind the main,
Casting a shadow, then returned again;
And all that time he never seemed to see.
Like friendly ghosts we moved invisibly.

He didn't want the water or the bread,
We offered in slow motion with a dread
Of sudden change of starting apprehension.
Other visions occupied his head.

And so it often is when love we have to offer
Fails to fulfill the needs of one another.
Only the earth and trees could still the yearning,
That held him homeward past all interfering.

Transmigration

A catastrophe has occurred in the night.
A ringtailed raccoon has met with an accident.
His former habitation lies in the road, enveloped
in stillness, haunted by crows.
Where he himself has gone nobody knows.

The New Senate Office Building

I

You can plaster on the marble. You can splatter on the paint.
You can castigate a member who would exercise restraint.
You can stress a lofty ceiling that is sure to catch the eye.
You can build a mighty tower that impinges on the sky.
You can shine a thousand windows til they glitter in the sun
But, (the thing that really matters) is there work that's getting done?

II

You can panel every office with mahogany and teak.
You can hang a sign on any door, "do not disturb, asleep."
You can build a new gymnasium, and add a turkish bath,
To fill the need for sweating out the mornings aftermath,
But when you spread a carpet that's eleven inches thick,
It can slow the speed of progress; it can even jam the stick.
Oh it's nice to have three dining rooms, a bar and kitchenette,
It's nice to sit and smoke cigars whenever you have et
It's nice to have a service that is coming on the run,
But, (the thing that really matters) is there work that's getting done?

III

Oh there's something in the gizzard of a Yankee politic
That hates the waste of money for the sake of looking slick,

That wants a dollar value for a dollar that is spent,
That remembers what he came to do, the reasons he was sent.
Now don't misunderstand me, sure a man must have his fun
But, (the thing that really matters) is there work that's getting done?

Martin Luther King

Aching heat, tension and pre-storm stillness,
Where one dry leaf suddenly spins like a windmill,
A single splatter in the dust. The rumble of distant anger,
Before the broken, golden fire strikes,
And the heavens burst out crying, exploding tears,
Washing away the worst, bringing the evening sky.
Is this the way it is for those who must
Hold love in the outstretched hand before they die?

Corn Flowers

The corn flowers at the roadways edge
Do not succumb to dust or sun or rain.
Growing along a margin or a ledge,
They have their say, indifferent to pain.
You can not pick them though. They fade too fast.
They have to struggle if they're going to last.

Prometheus

In summer the fireplace is dead,
Housing a yellow paper long since read,
Supporting charred logs that never found their way,
Through fire and smoke to reach a better day.
On top perhaps a bunch of faded flowers,
Watered by sooty drops from thunder showers,
Ignored except by dustpan's clang and clatter,
A place where no one goes, and nothing matters,
Until the changing season brings desire,
To prove that dross can speak with tongues of fire.

The Prophet

I

A single maple bough of gold and red,
Unwelcomed interposition in July,
Like an unwanted visit from the dead,
Disturbs the comfort of a summer sky.

II

Green hills, fat clouds and cows meandering,
Swirls of yellow butterflies philandering,
The season's semblance of eternity,
Behold a prophet of adversity.

III

Does this sign of death in life,
Emblem of wind and rain and strife,
Foretell the ending of the story,
Or does it speak of future glory?

"Old Gregarious"

When we go for a run my dog keeps coming back to me
  for confirmation,
From time to time, pausing in his exploration
  of a wider territory,
Before reversing at full speed, impatient, disappearing,
Into dimensions past my perservering.
I wonder at his need to reestablish ties,
With one whose passage underneath the skies
Progresses with as little variation,
As a string of freight cars in a railroad station,
Unless perhaps he has a need like me,
To mingle and enjoy good company.

The Commuters

A squirrel is running across the road.
His cheeks protruding a summer load,
That's got to be buried far and deep
In a secret place for winter keep.
I hope he makes it, the traffic hums
Like an angry hive when a stranger comes.
I hope he makes it and doesn't lie,
His paws outstretched to the autumn sky,
His coat bespattered, his tail all wet,
His guts bright red for the crows to get.
I hope he makes it and doesn't die
For the sake of putting some nuggets by.

Distance = Rate x Time

I

We left the house behind us in the dunes.
The truck had picked a quarrel with the road.
Explosive language, mingled with a growl
Swaying and protesting at the load.

II

Two rutted tracks defined the letter Z.
Across a pancake Isle from sea to bay.
Golden rod went down on bended knee,
Wounded, and abandoned where they lay.

III

Increments of time don't coincide.
The mile between the firs was many hours,
Loaded with love, the ache and pull of tide,
The message and the singing of the flowers.

IV

Though distance equals rate times time,
A thousand miles in flight is often sped,
Without the recognition that they're mine.
I have a different timepiece in my head.

September Swim

"If you throw your head back,
And look straight up, keeping your feet to windward
   in the rollers,
You'll see a lot more stars than just the evening star,
Above the orange ingot in the west.
A comet might become unleashed and, sliding down
   the sky,
Immerse itself in lonely seas, beyond the farthest
   wave," I said.
"It's getting cold. I think we should go in," she said.
   And so we did.

Q. E. D.

Quiet emphasis of mountains.
Indifference of the sea,
Impervious constellations,
Independence of a tree.

Lonely hills and stubborn waters,
Cosmogony of stars,
Their immensity would drown us,
Were it not that love is ours.

October

I cast all day from a barrier reef,
But all I hooked was a maple leaf,
Red against my silver lure
As it bounced an irregular course to shore.
The leaf in my hand was smooth and wet,
With a crust of salt like a coronet,
Till I dropped it onto a stone below
Where the sun could dry, and the wind might blow
It back to the swells, and the autumn haze
To finish its journey and end its days.

Dogs

I

My wife keeps dogs in the bedroom.
She says that they need it for sleep,
That elsewhere they might become nervous,
Might even go bark at a thief.

II

My wife keeps dogs in the bedroom,
Their presence is hard to eschew.
If they're not knocking over a table,
They're quietly chewing a shoe.

III

My wife keeps dogs in the bedroom.
They growl and they snarl in the night
As if perhaps they're indulging
In canine debate, or a fight.

IV

My wife keeps dogs in the bedroom.
Their discretion is open to doubt.
If something's about to get started
They're likely to scratch to get out.

V

My wife keeps dogs in the bedroom,
And if I emit a mild curse
She relegates me to the doghouse,
An anthropomorphic reverse.

Love Poem

Awaking and looking out of the window,
I see a maple with arms akimbo,
Others outstretched, some amputations,
Some junctions hiding destinations,
The whole inclining toward the south
Rubbing shoulders with the house,
Leaning into autumn rain,
Scraping twigs on window pane.
I wonder how this simple sight
Can fill me full of grave delight.
I wonder how such things may be,
That love can linger in a tree,
Until I think the memory
Of one who watched the tree with me.

Same As Ever

I

Antennae probing, reaching furthest stars.
Searching deep across the cosmic wind,
Hello out there, and tell us who you are,
And where the giant voice that speaks your mind.

II

Certain it is an answer will return,
Nor cause surprise to hear our neighbors say,
Their need is also love, the same as ours,
Though born again a billion miles away.

The Pilgrim

Nobody makes it to the top without a pack on his back,
You can't even get through the foothills
No matter how brightly the morning sun shines on the
    distant peaks,
Without the burdens that round your shoulders and
    push your eyes into the ground,
The inferiorities, anxieties, compulsions, obsessions,
    self-prostitutions.
But you didn't ask for them. You didn't say,
    "These I can carry."
They were shovelled onto you by unseen hands in a
    country you never knew, or can't remember,
Coming out of darkness, evil, hate, piled onto you
    without permission.
But this is how it is—this is the situation—these
    are the hazards, the obstacles.
And sometimes, as with Job, there aren't many options.
    But there's always one.
You may not be able to make it to the top, not for a
    long time,
But the stance you take, the internal response is yours.
The choice, the decision, what you make of it, how you
    choose to look at it
Can sunder the chains, splinter the bars,
Destroy the appearance, consolidate that which you are,
Help you to shout through the din.
Though he slay me still will I trust in him.

Trees

I

The trees have quit their autumn dance,
And stand as in a holy trance,
Black against the somber sky,
Waiting, standing, silently.

II

Waiting to receive the snow,
All their summer green let go,
All their joys and all their laughter
Lost or gone to their hereafter.

III

Patient against the persistence of the snow,
Enduring against the thunder of the storm,
Hiding the secret life in deepest roots,
Waiting the time they know when sap is born.

Obituary

Death of a dog descended on our house tonight,
Along with a November storm that doused the light,
And left us standing there remembering how
He had a way of setting things to right.
Wag of a tail or barking salutation,
Union at night or morning separation,
Presided over with a loving care,
That asked no more than his accustomed share,
Of recognition or communication,
Nothing, I say, beyond his humble station,
Remembering this, and how my wife
Would hold a piece of toast to make him speak,
I thanked the wind, that made the dark, that
    hid the wet,
That furrowed down my cheek.

Dawn

There's a pony loose in Matheson's meadow.
     He must have got out in the night.
The December grass is brown and brittle,
     But some of it must be right.
He's browsing away as hard as he can
Though his casual posture's a bit of a sham;
And he knows, though he's stretching his usual span,
And wants to stay free as long as he can,
That he'll be returned to his proper place,
An innocent look on his furry face,
His breath like steam from a fireman's hose,
Discharging its separate way from his nose,
While the sun at the edge of the field looks over
the back of a boy and a pony's shoulder.

December Twenty-Third

An early morn, with mist and snow,
And out of the wet the voice of a crow,
Invisible there in his lofty station,
Establishing lines of communication.

Winter Poem

The tiny, gentle, falling, drifting flakes
Can change direction in a moment's span;
Aimless, without a purpose or a plan
Shifting throughout the arc a compass makes,
Like motes or bits of dust a sunbeam holds,
Disturbed by idle motion of a hand,
Flipped back and forth between the golden band,
Hither and yon before us in the cold.
The pirouettes respond to every breeze,
Sashaying over housetops, over trees,
But still a question can not help arise.
Who wrote the tune above us in the skies?
Whose is the theme to which the slanting song
Of reckless, shifting winter should belong?

Back to the Beginning

Do you lie awake in the early gloom
Before the dawn in an empty room,
Burrowing down from the winter chill,
Tasting snow on the windowsill,
Hearing your heartbeat through the springs
The pulse and rhythm of living things,
Beating steadily sounding clear,
Like a stream intent to be gone from here,
And down from a hillside running free
To its ocean source of identity?

Epitaph

God wants us to die gently in our sleep, in old age,
    after many sunny days
Built by a life of work, a life of praise.
God does not countenance the ravages, the ills,
The mind an empty tower where at will
Demons will be howling at all hours,
Tearing the soul, dismembering the powers.
God wants the congregation of the years
Sanctified by laughter, solemnized by love,
With, held in reserve for sympathy alone, the tears.

Skating

The Big Dipper isn't much for holding anything
On a January night tumbled against the horizon
Almost upside down to finger the Northern star,
But the shine's enough to make fat shadows on the ice
From trees that line themselves along the shore,
And if you've never skated on a pond, tucked in behind
    the dunes,
Or felt the salt north wind bemuse your eye,
You ought to ask yourself the reason why.

Afterwards

After the storm the clouds still linger,
Making a sullen departure, a corrugated iron roof,
Encasing the scene, secret, diminutive.
The earth of course so very pure, except where fallen branches
Make questions in the snow, awaits the advent of the blue,
Or even the possibility that a star shine through.

The Long View

The shadows on an aging face
Do not arise in outer space.
Their origin is from within,
From passion, pain and maybe sin.
But steadfast for the longer run,
The eyes themselves do not succumb,
But fasten onto farthest stars
Looking for truth between the bars.

Too Cold

I

It was too cold to snow
The earth was hard as glass and twice as brittle.
Because it could not bend, it broke a little
And found no where to go.

II

And yet the ponderous clouds above the wood
Huddled their shoulders with a grey intent
To squeeze at least one tiny flake below,
To drift across a frozen firmament.

The Conservationist

A nonagenarian with the hearing aid, the thick glasses,
    and a tipped pelvis,
Has an appointment. It is nothing really. He feels fine,
    just a checkup.
But you can see it is an event. He is spic and span. His
    cane has a new red rubber ending.
And what he says with his presence is a proclamation, a
    hallelujah,
An acknowledgement of abundance, the individual kingdom,
The texture of living, so wonderful as to justify conservation
    down to the last iota.
His presence shouts louder than an avalanche of angels,
    or the beating of drums.

The Need

It didn't snow that year, not till the end of January.
The wonder was, what had become of all that sky vocabulary,
All those tiny white answers to prayers, gently responding,
Constructing stillness, after their soft bombarding?
Too much nakedness isn't good.
The earth was old and that was understood,
But it needed to be enveloped in the white,
If spring was ever to come and make it right.

March

A lawn scrubbed clean by wind and rain
As if someone had snatched the counterpane
Of snow that lay the night before,
Like a polar sea from door to door.
But there's nothing else in the black and tan
Of empty fields and winter span
That says it's time to change the scene,
Or bring on melting where ice has been.

Reese Alsop

ALTHOUGH able to point to a commendable record in the practice of medicine for the last thirty years, including chairmanship of the department of medicine at Huntington Hospital and assistant professor at New York University, Dr. Alsop's earlier career must be described as checkered. In his youth, like Churchill and Tolstoy, he was "scandalously desultory." Expelled from Groton School at the age of thirteen for academic ineptitude, it required a pedagogical miracle at a less demanding institution to effect matriculation at Harvard, with the same class from which he had been jettisoned. Once there, however, his natural indolence reasserted itself so that by the end of his freshman year he had achieved the standing of dropped freshman on probation, a last gasp category.

Always a scrambler, he stepped out of the pocket and recovered again, to graduate with his class this time majoring in philosophy.

But there were further difficulties. Gainful employment escaped him. He found himself in a buyer's market, and turned flounderingly to the stage. Here success awaited so that with a leading role on Broadway, and the road, sufficient funds accrued to defray the costs of Columbia Presbyterian Medical School.

In spite of these questionable beginnings the years have been kind to Dr. Alsop. He has been happy, and has remained steadfast in his love for the profession with only an occasional dalliance as evidenced by *Back Talk*, two childrens books published by Dodd Mead & Company and a series of humorous articles in *Havard* magazine. Other efforts have included writings on medical subjects in the *New England Journal of Medicine*, *Life* magazine and the *Readers Digest*.

Reese Alsop jogs. In fact he started jogging twenty five years ago. Glancing backward over his shoulder at the years with their varied accumulations, he wonders sometimes whether he has not always been running scared, while still, on another level, acknowledging "the means of grace and the hope of glory."